Until they are about
five years old,
BALD EAGLES have
BROWN HEADS.

weird but true!

★ USA ★

300
FASCINATING FACTS
ABOUT THE FIFTY STATES

NATIONAL GEOGRAPHIC
WASHINGTON, D.C.

sometimes **EAT SHARKS** in Florida.

5

One Washington, D.C., Metro stop is **21 stories** deep.

In 1969, **530 million people** watched American astronauts **walk on the moon—** **five times more** than watched the 2018 Super Bowl.

Colonial
Americans
**made
candy**
out of
potatoes.

The
distance between
Russia AND Alaska
at their closest point is about
twice the length of the
Golden Gate Bridge.

If Alaska were cut in half, each half would still be bigger than Texas.

8

Nine **Yankee Stadiums** could fit inside Minnesota's **Mall of America.**

I ♥ COLORADO!

Louisiana hosts a **four-day mud festival** known as **Mudfest.**

On average, **CATS IN COLORADO LIVE TWO YEARS LONGER** than cats in other states, one study found.

Montana has **more cows** than people.

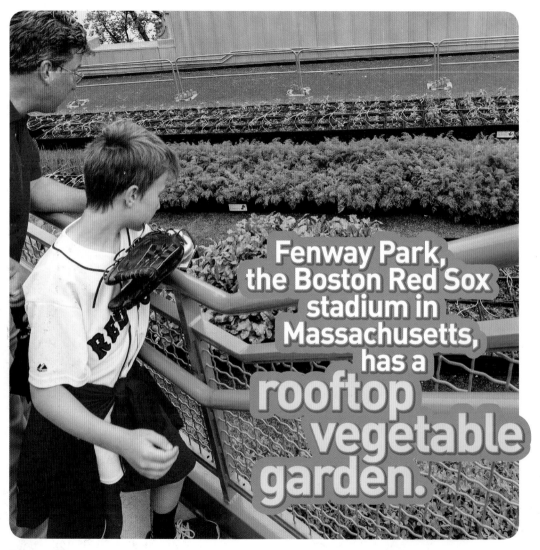

Fenway Park, the Boston Red Sox stadium in Massachusetts, has a **rooftop vegetable garden.**

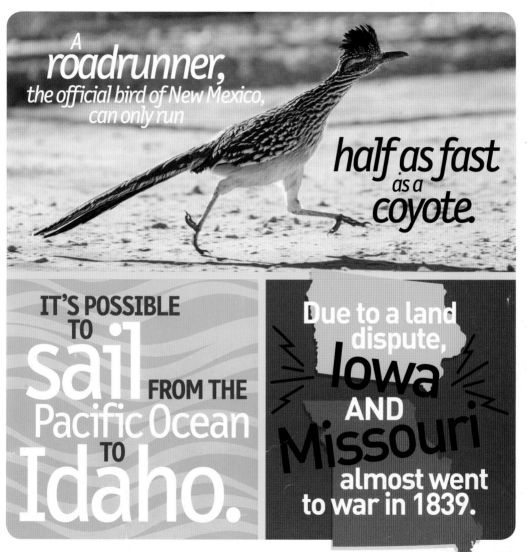

A **roadrunner,** the official bird of New Mexico, can only run **half as fast** as a **coyote.**

IT'S POSSIBLE TO **sail** FROM THE Pacific Ocean TO **Idaho.**

Due to a land dispute, **Iowa** AND **Missouri** almost went to war in 1839.

13

THREE OF THE FIRST FIVE U.S. PRESIDENTS DIED ON **JULY 4.**

NO U.S. PRESIDENT HAS EVER **DIED IN MAY.**

EIGHT PRESIDENTS HAVE BEEN BORN IN **VIRGINIA,** THE MOST OF ANY STATE.

In 2015, the U.S. made an average of more than **two movies a day.**

Some people return LAVA ROCKS they have taken from Hawaii because they believe they

CAUSE BAD LUCK.

The only way to reach the post office in Point Roberts, Washington, is by **DRIVING THROUGH CANADA FIRST.**

Welcome to **CANADA**

In 1948, two men were arrested in Connecticut for selling **bad pickles.**

"*fresh*" *pickles*

17

The United States averages **1,250** tornadoes every year— about 10 times more than any other country.

Every March, Texas averages more than one tornado a day.

The
root beer float
was once called the
black cow.

The city of **Los Angeles** was founded in 1781, **NINE YEARS** before Washington, D.C.

When you drive **45 miles an hour** (72 km/h) over a section of highway in New Mexico, the vibrations from your car's wheels play **"America the Beautiful."**

Florida IS THE FLATTEST U.S. STATE.

More than **200 languages** are spoken in **New York City.**

The state **"FLOWER"** of Maine is the **WHITE PINECONE.**

Tomato JUICE IS OHIO'S STATE DRINK.

Every year, more than **100 million passengers** fly through the airport in Atlanta, Georgia— the **busiest in the world.**

About one-third of the veggies that U.S. kids eat are **potatoes.**

23

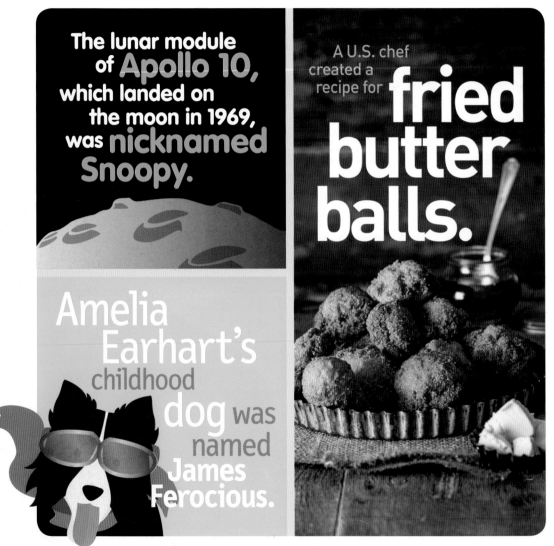

The lunar module of **Apollo 10,** which landed on the moon in 1969, was **nicknamed Snoopy.**

A U.S. chef created a recipe for **fried butter balls.**

Amelia Earhart's childhood **dog** was named **James Ferocious.**

24

ENGLISH MUFFINS originated in New York, not England.

America's top five ice-cream flavors are

vanilla

chocolate

cookies and cream

mint chocolate chip and

chocolate chip cookie dough

a survey found.

27

One of the MOST REQUESTED PHOTOS from the National Archives is of President RICHARD NIXON shaking hands with ELVIS.

The American flag's official colors are Old Glory Red, White, and Old Glory Blue.

The **Expedition Everest** roller coaster at Disney World **cost $100 million** to build.

The United States is the only country where both

alligators

Sarah Polk, wife of President James K. Polk, **BANNED DANCING** in the **WHITE HOUSE.**

Posted
NO DANCING

and

crocodiles

can be found in the same location.

Before he was
a famous musician,

Elvis Presley

drove a **DELIVERY** truck.

ON THE LIBERTY BELL, PENNSYLVANIA IS SPELLED

A **Saint Bernard** in South Dakota has the world's **longest dog tongue** —more than seven inches long. (18 cm)

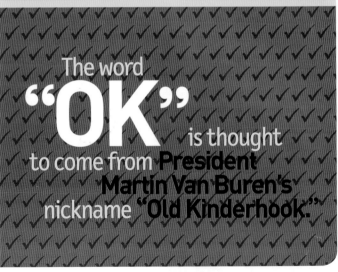

The word **"OK"** is thought to come from **President Martin Van Buren's** nickname **"Old Kinderhook."**

The Angel Oak tree near Charleston, South Carolina, shades an area the size of **THREE AND A HALF BASKETBALL COURTS.**

A BIRDCAGE

A GOLF TEE

A MAILBOX

A PITCHFORK

THE TOWN OF CASEY, ILLINOIS, HAS THE

WORLD'S LARGEST

STATUES OF ...

KNITTING NEEDLES

A ROCKING CHAIR

WIND CHIMES

WOODEN SHOES

35

A prehistoric mound in Ohio—which is shaped like a snake swallowing an egg—is more than 1,400 feet (425 m) long.

There is a
UFO WATCHTOWER

in
San Luis Valley, Colorado.

President Franklin D. Roosevelt **DISLIKED** the number **13**.

In Massachusetts, it's illegal to have **exploding golf balls.**

A female American bullfrog lays up to **20,000** eggs.

California's San Andreas Fault moves at about the same rate as your fingernails grow.

Before Phoenix, Arizona, became an official city, it was called **PUMPKINVILLE.**

A rabbit in Los Angeles can **slam-dunk** a mini basketball in a mini hoop seven times in 60 seconds.

BINI THE BUN

41

THE TRUNK OF THE WORLD'S LARGEST TREE, LOCATED IN CALIFORNIA, WEIGHS AS MUCH

42

Nutty Narrows Bridge in Longview, Washington, was built so **squirrels can safely cross** a busy road.

Independence Day is July 4, but delegates from the 13 colonies VOTED FOR INDEPENDENCE ON JULY 2.

A mile-long (1.3-km) island RECENTLY FORMED off North Carolina's OUTER BANKS.

A man in Findlay, Illinois, built a three-story brick tower for his **34 goats.**

It takes about **90 days** for a drop of water to travel the length of the Mississippi River.

THERE IS ENOUGH WATER IN LAKE SUPERIOR TO FLOOD ALL OF NORTH AND SOUTH AMERICA IN ONE FOOT OF WATER.

(30 cm)

One in eight Americans eats pizza on any given day.

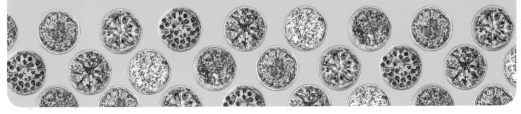

Cindy, a greyhound from Florida, holds the world record for **highest jump by a dog:** five feet eight inches. (172.7 cm)

42 percent of Americans believe in GHOSTS.

Salamanders in the United States range in size from a paper clip to longer than a baseball bat.

You can walk through a three-story stained-glass globe in Boston, Massachusetts.

Thor's Well,

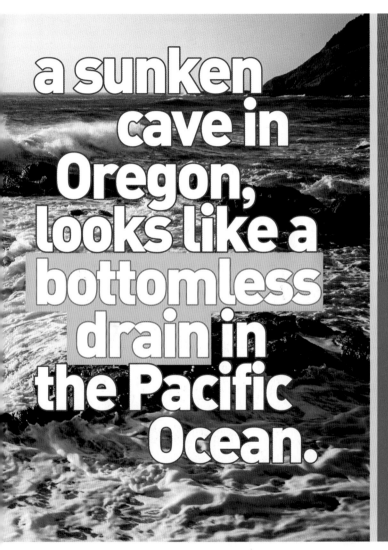

a sunken cave in Oregon, looks like a bottomless drain in the Pacific Ocean.

ABRAHAM LINCOLN is in the National WRESTLING Hall of Fame.

President Chester A. Arthur AUCTIONED OFF a pair of President ABRAHAM LINCOLN'S PANTS to help pay for White House renovations.

In California's Mono Lake, limestone formations called tufa towers are **THREE STORIES TALL.**

An American REVOLUTIONARY WAR **BATTLE FLAG** sold for more than $12 million —the MOST EXPENSIVE FLAG ever sold at auction.

Hawaii IS THE ONLY STATE THAT GROWS **coffee beans**.

The **largest private home** in the United States, the Biltmore Estate

More than **700 flavors** of soda are sold at a Los Angeles soda pop store.

Most of **Mount Rushmore** was carved with **dynamite.**

The **Pledge of Allegiance** was written for a magazine to help **sell subscriptions.**

The bark of giant sequoia trees, found only in California, grows up to **two feet thick.**

(0.6 m)

You can **DIG** for **DIAMONDS** in a crater in Arkansas and **KEEP** what **YOU FIND.**

THE DOG on the **CRACKER JACK** box is named **BINGO.**

The territory of **American Samoa** is closer to **Australia** than to **Hawaii.**

A Native American legend says that the creases in Wyoming's **Devils Tower** were **clawed** by a bear.

Jell-O
is the official
state snack of
UTAH.

George Washington Carver invented **300** uses for peanuts, including soap, hand lotion, and glue.

A HALF-SIZE MODEL OF THE LEANING TOWER OF PISA WAS BUILT IN ILLINOIS TO STORE WATER.

VERMONT MAPLE SYRUP HAS ABOUT

THE SAME AMOUNT OF CALCIUM AS WHOLE MILK.

A bird found only in the U.S., **THE GREATER PRAIRIE CHICKEN,** stomps its feet and makes **LOW BOOMING SOUNDS** to attract mates.

The Colorado State Fair holds a **pet rock Olympics,** including a prize for the **best dressed rock.**

President George H. W. Bush **BANNED BROCCOLI** from Air Force One.

ICK!

67

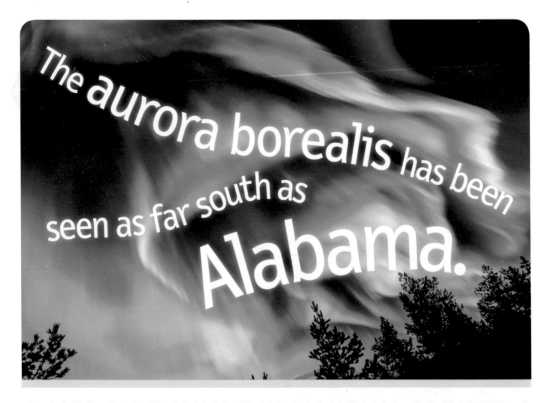

The aurora borealis has been seen as far south as Alabama.

A 1959 EARTHQUAKE IN MONTANA CREATED A FIVE-MILE-LONG LAKE.

(8-km)

A building in Nashville, Tennessee, has towers that look like the ears of **BATMAN'S MASK.**

THE ONLY APPLE NATIVE TO THE UNITED STATES IS THE CRAB APPLE.

69

The
Washington
National
Cathedral
has a
Darth
Vader
gargoyle.

Some 1954 **lunch boxes** featuring the American character **Superman** can sell for **$20,000.**

At the North Dakota State Fair, visitors can compete in a **grease-covered-watermelon race.**

Google was started in a
garage.

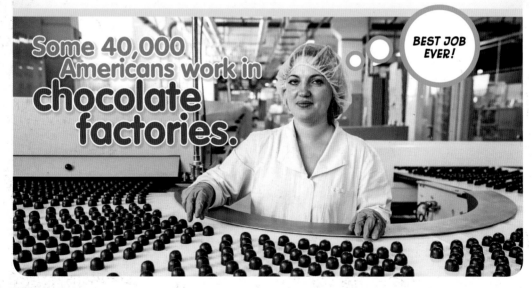

Some 40,000 Americans work in **chocolate factories.**

BEST JOB EVER!

The heat tiles on NASA's space shuttles were made from high-grade sand.

California leads all states in UFO sightings.

A study found that Americans report more UFO sightings on the **Fourth of July** than on any other day.

Wildflowers found in parts of the Pacific Northwest are called long-beard hawkweed, poet's shooting star, Columbia kittentail, and northern wormwood.

A chewy peanut-and-caramel treat known as **Squirrel Nut Zippers** was created in Massachusetts in 1890.

Golfers at a course in Fort Fairfield, Maine, can hit balls **across the Canadian border.**

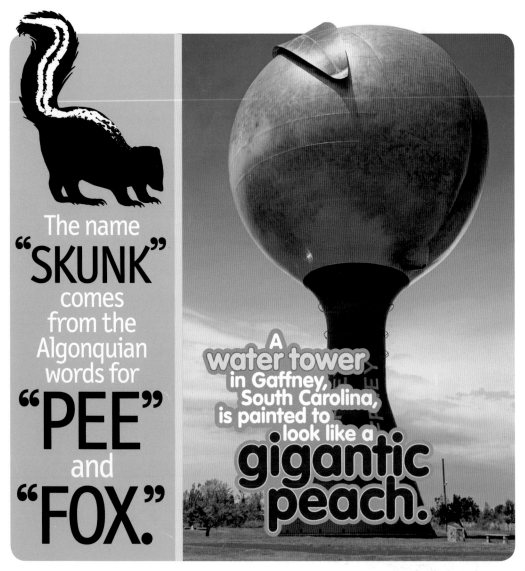

The name "SKUNK" comes from the Algonquian words for "PEE" and "FOX."

A water tower in Gaffney, South Carolina, is painted to look like a gigantic peach.

There is a **toilet-seat art** museum in San Antonio, Texas.

BEFORE **CHICKEN MCNUGGETS,** MCDONALD'S IN THE U.S. BRIEFLY SOLD **"ONION NUGGETS."**

A LIBRARY BOOK checked out by George Washington was returned to a New York City library 221 YEARS LATE.

You can stay inside a **beagle-shaped hotel** in Idaho.

80

Legend says that anyone who enters the CAVE OF THE EVIL SPIRIT beside Niagara Falls will be cursed with **bad luck.**

California scientists modeled a **solar cell** —used to turn sunlight into electricity— after a **fly's eye.**

PRESIDENT
ABRAHAM
LINCOLN
KEPT LETTERS

IN HIS STOVEPIPE HAT.

The **Virginia opossum** can have as many as **20 babies** in a litter.

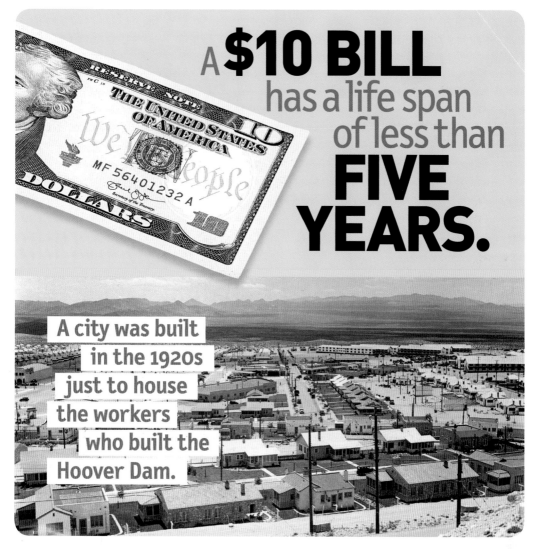

A **$10 BILL** has a life span of less than **FIVE YEARS.**

A city was built in the 1920s just to house the workers who built the Hoover Dam.

85

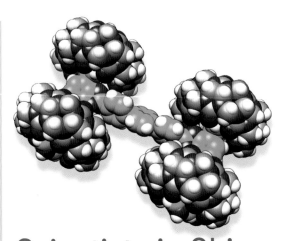

At the Georgia State Fair, the **winning pig** in the pig races **gets an Oreo cookie.**

Scientists in Ohio created a miniature "**MONSTER TRUCK**" out of FIVE MOLECULES.

35% of Americans say they have eaten PIE for BREAKFAST, a survey found.

A U.S. deputy named

BASS REEVES

was said to have arrested more than 3,000 lawbreakers—and was

the inspiration for the Lone Ranger.

The world's largest
BALL OF STAMPS,
which is in Nebraska, weighs more than 600 pounds— (272 kg)
it's as heavy as two giant pandas.

At a restaurant in Kentucky, people try to eat a **five-pound** (2-kg) **hamburger** in less than an hour.

A construction crew in Colorado unearthed a **66-MILLION-YEAR-OLD** *TOROSAURUS*, a relative of *Triceratops*.

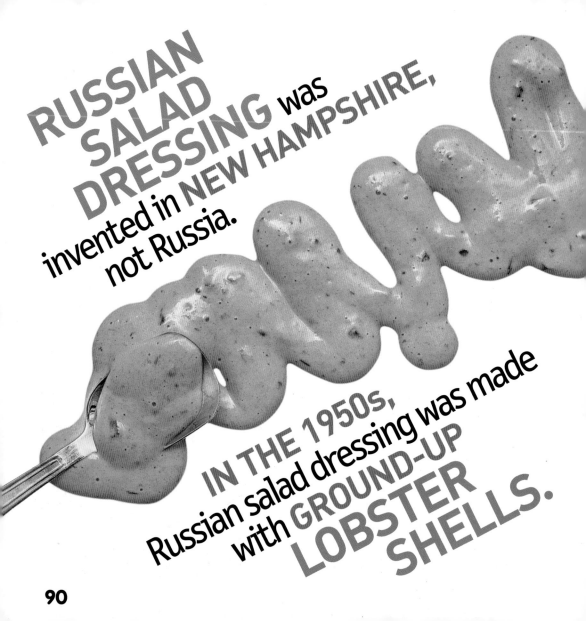

RUSSIAN SALAD DRESSING was invented in **NEW HAMPSHIRE,** not Russia.

IN THE 1950s, Russian salad dressing was made with **GROUND-UP LOBSTER SHELLS.**

The **ATOM** was **FIRST SPLIT** beneath the **FOOTBALL STANDS** at the University of Chicago, in Illinois.

In ancient Alaska, diapers were made of moss.

HOT DOGS got their name in the United States from being known as **"DACHSHUND SAUSAGES"** in Germany.

IT TOOK TWO PEOPLE MORE THAN **400 hours** TO BUILD A MODEL OF THE **Liberty Bell**

WITH **Lego bricks.**

When Twinkies were invented in Chicago, Illinois, in 1930, you could buy two for just five cents.

Twinkies were originally filled with banana cream, but a U.S. banana shortage during World War II forced a switch to vanilla cream.

Puerto Rico's Gran Telescopio Canarias, one of the **largest telescopes in the world,** is taller than two giraffes stacked on top of each other.

EARLY AMERICAN COLONISTS MADE "COFFINS" —PIES COOKED IN LONG PANS.

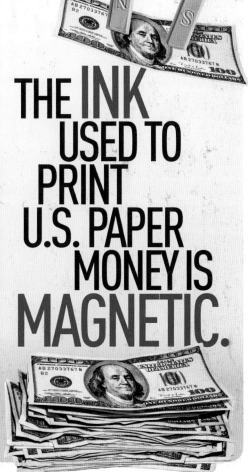

THE **INK** USED TO PRINT U.S. PAPER MONEY IS **MAGNETIC.**

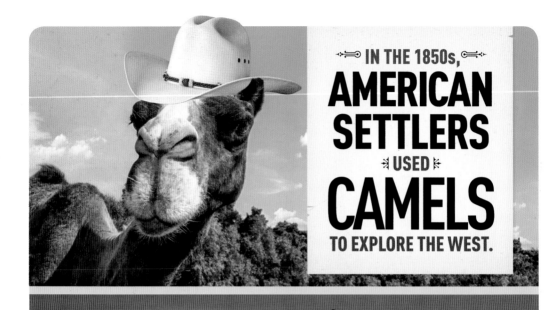

IN THE 1850s, **AMERICAN SETTLERS** USED **CAMELS** TO EXPLORE THE WEST.

A **nine-year-old** boy exploring in New Mexico's Organ Mountains **tripped** over a *Stegomastodon* fossil.

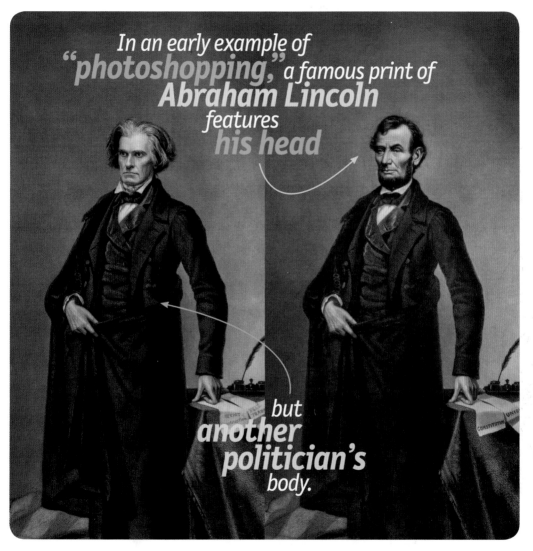

In an early example of "**photoshopping**," a famous print of **Abraham Lincoln** features *his head* but **another politician's** body.

Oregon harvests about **FIVE MILLION CHRISTMAS TREES** every year—more than any other state.

The Virgin Islands is the only place in the U.S. where people drive on the **left side** of the road.

MCDONALD'S is sometimes called **Mickey D's** in the United States, **Macca's** in Australia, and **McDo** in France.

It takes **570 GALLONS** of paint to cover the outside of the **WHITE HOUSE.**

(2,158 L)

★American★Paints★
WHITE HOUSE WHITE

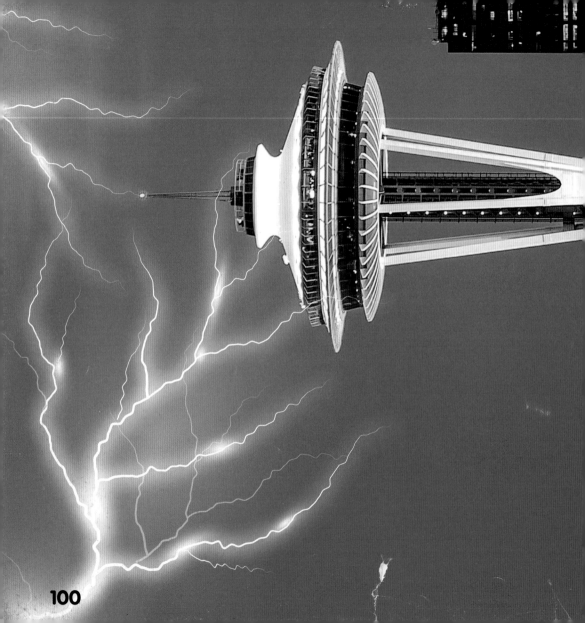

There are **24** **lightning rods** on the roof of the Seattle Space Needle to help it withstand lightning strikes.

70 percent of American pet owners sign **their pet's** name to greeting cards, a survey found.

President George H. W. Bush **celebrated** his **90th** birthday by **skydiving.**

TEXAS'S LARGEST WIND FARM IS 4.5 TIMES THE SIZE OF MANHATTAN.

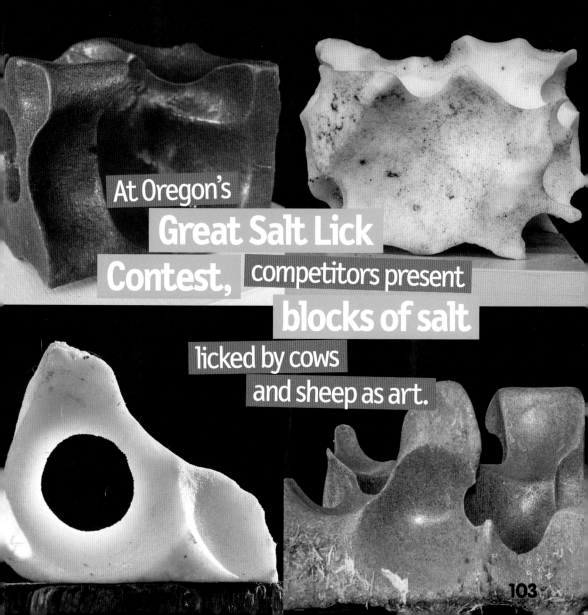

At Oregon's **Great Salt Lick Contest,** competitors present **blocks of salt** licked by cows and sheep as art.

103

Buzz Aldrin took a
SPACE "SELFIE"
in 1966.

In 1934, dust from Texas traveled so far that it coated ships' decks in the Atlantic Ocean.

McNally Plaza in New York City is **SO SMALL** that only a few people can fit in it.

Minnesota has nearly **12,000 lakes** that are each larger than **three and a half soccer fields.**

San Francisco's famous **fog** is nicknamed **Karl.**

One desk drawer on the U.S. Senate floor is **always stocked with candy.**

Ghost fireflies
of the southeastern
United States
glow blue.

A Miss American Vampire contest was held in **California** in 1970.

You could **drive across** Rhode Island, the **smallest state,** in just one hour.

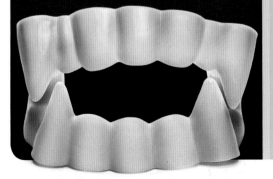

A Wisconsin corn maze was designed in the shape of a trilobite, an arthropod that crawled seafloors 250 million years ago.

The North American Wood Ape Conservancy in Texas researches

Bigfoot

sightings.

Bigfoot is also known as Woolly Booger in Texas.

BOOGER XING

THE WORLD'S LARGEST CHICKEN NUGGET, MADE IN NEW JERSEY, WAS AS BIG AS 720 NUGGETS COMBINED.

White House staff used **snowmen** to **play a prank** on President Barack Obama.

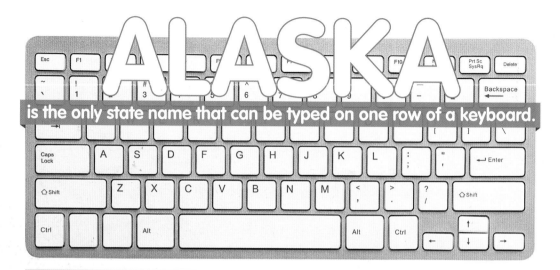

ALASKA

is the only state name that can be typed on one row of a keyboard.

An **Illinois man** set a **world record** by eating six **peanut butter** and **jelly sandwiches** in one minute.

115

In Chicago, Illinois, the Tribune Building contains rocks from ...

THE GREAT PYRAMID OF KHUFU IN GIZA, EGYPT

THE MOON

ABRAHAM LINCOLN'S TOMB IN SPRINGFIELD, ILLINOIS

THE ALAMO IN SAN ANTONIO, TEXAS

THE COLOSSEUM IN ROME, ITALY

117

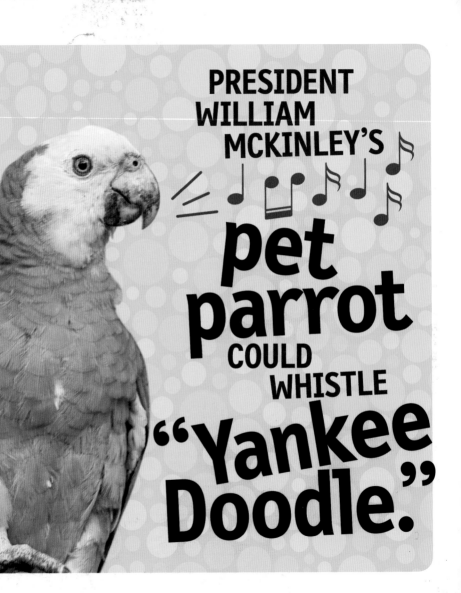

PRESIDENT WILLIAM MCKINLEY'S pet parrot COULD WHISTLE "Yankee Doodle."

Kool-Aid, invented in Nebraska, was originally called **FRUIT SMACK.**

Mortimer was Walt Disney's original choice for **Mickey Mouse's** first name.

CALIFORNIA HAS AN **official state dinosaur:** a **duck-billed** PLANT-EATER THAT LIVED **66 million years** AGO.

THE CITY OF **PORTLAND, OREGON,** WAS NAMED IN A **COIN TOSS** —IT HAD A **FIFTY-FIFTY CHANCE** OF BECOMING BOSTON, OREGON.

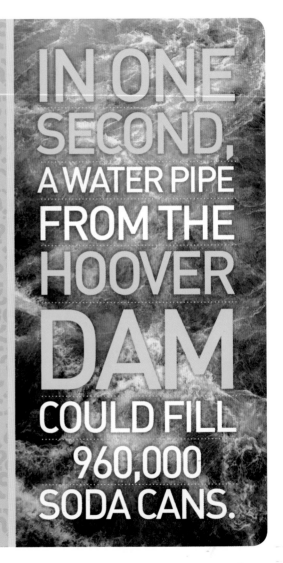

IN ONE SECOND, A WATER PIPE FROM THE HOOVER DAM COULD FILL 960,000 SODA CANS.

The Rumble Ponies, the Yard Goats, the Flying Squirrels, and the Crawdads are minor league American baseball teams.

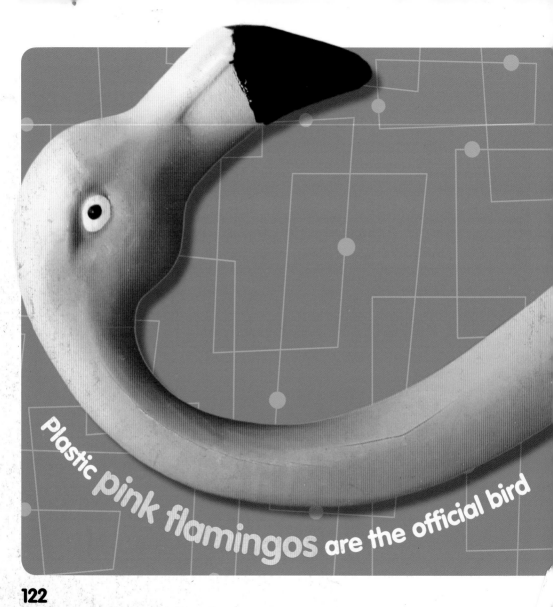

Plastic pink flamingos are the official bird

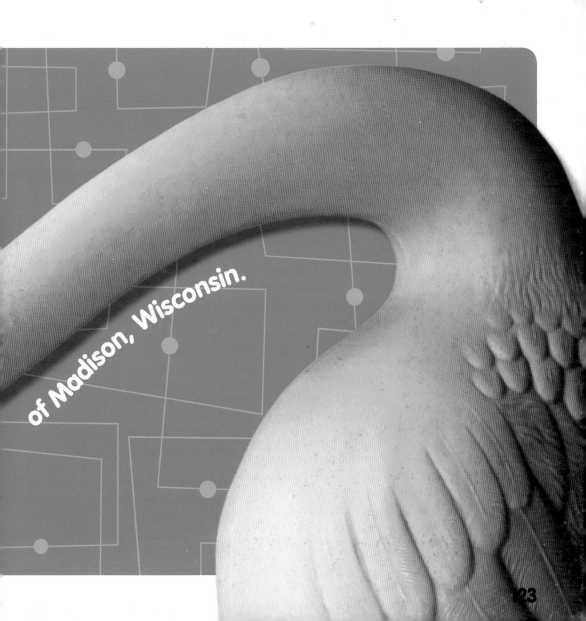

of Madison, Wisconsin.

FOUND IN THE U.S., THE GRASSHOPPER MOUSE **screeches like a wolf** BEFORE IT **attacks its prey.**

OINK?

Humuhumunukunukuāpuaʻa
—the official state fish
of Hawaii—means **"with a snout like a pig."**

During the Civil War, soldiers ate **peanut brittle** as part of their rations.

The Wonderful Wizard of Oz

was originally titled

From Kansas to Fairyland.

THE LIBRARY OF CONGRESS ADDS ABOUT **12,000 ITEMS** TO ITS COLLECTION **EACH DAY.**

NASA's logo is known as the "**meatball.**"

Making *Captain EO*, a movie shown at Disney parks, cost **$1.76 million** for each **minute** of the film.

127

Employees at a **popcorn factory** in Illinois created a **3,423-pound** (1,553-kg) popcorn

ball
about the size of a
small hippo.

STUBBY, A DOG WHO SERVED IN WORLD WAR I, WAS AWARDED THE RANK OF UNITED STATES ARMY SERGEANT FOR FINDING A GERMAN SPY.

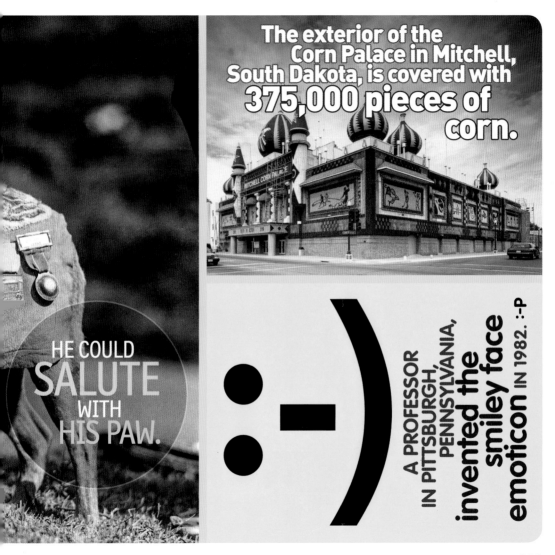

The exterior of the Corn Palace in Mitchell, South Dakota, is covered with **375,000** pieces of corn.

HE COULD **SALUTE** WITH HIS PAW.

:-)

A PROFESSOR IN PITTSBURGH, PENNSYLVANIA, invented the smiley face emoticon IN 1982. :-P

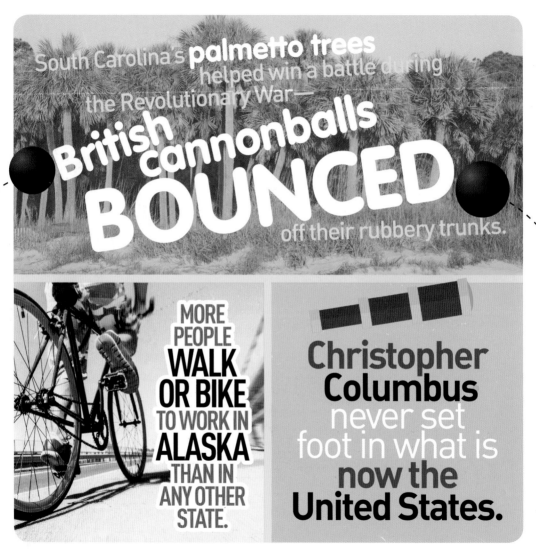

South Carolina's **palmetto trees** helped win a battle during the Revolutionary War—**British cannonballs BOUNCED** off their rubbery trunks.

MORE PEOPLE **WALK OR BIKE** TO WORK IN **ALASKA** THAN IN ANY OTHER STATE.

Christopher Columbus never set foot in what is **now the United States.**

SLICED BREAD
WAS 
BANNED
IN THE
UNITED STATES DURING
WORLD WAR II.

133

A museum in Chicago, Illinois, is home to Sue, the **largest** and

most complete **Tyrannosaurus rex** ever found.

THE MOST POPULAR CRAYON COLOR IN THE UNITED STATES IS BLUE.

A postal worker in Houston, Texas, built a **monument to oranges** using only objects he found around town.

President **William Henry Harrison's** inaugural address **lasted longer** than the movie *Finding Nemo.*

More than **20 DIFFERENT KINDS OF DINOSAURS** have been discovered **IN ONE GEOLOGICAL FORMATION** in parts of Montana, South Dakota, and North Dakota.

A **bathroom** in Las Vegas, Nevada, showcases a section of the **Berlin Wall.**

After the **DECLARATION of Independence** was first read to a crowd in Boston, Massachusetts, they burned statues **REPRESENTING Great Britain.**

BURGOO IS A TRADITIONAL KENTUCKY STEW.

On full-moon nights, a **moonbow** —a rainbow **caused by the moon**— sometimes appears at Kentucky's Cumberland Falls.

Green Bay, Wisconsin, is known as the toilet paper capital of the world.

Perforated toilet paper was invented in Albany, New York, in 1871.

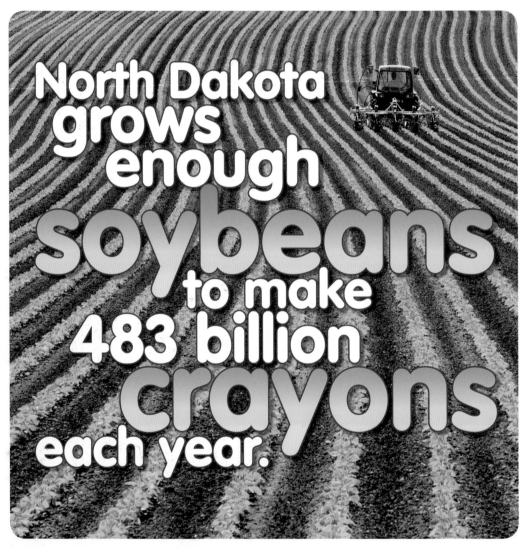

North Dakota grows enough soybeans to make 483 billion crayons each year.

Potato McTater,

a shih tzu from New York City, has more than **54,000 followers** on social media.

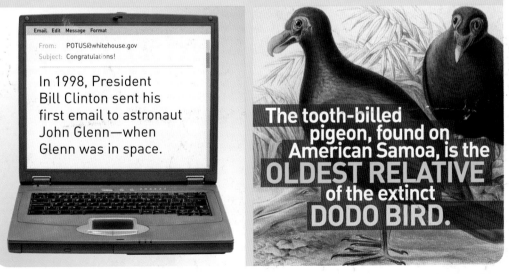

Email   Edit   Message   Format

From: POTUS@whitehouse.gov
Subject: Congratulations!

In 1998, President Bill Clinton sent his first email to astronaut John Glenn—when Glenn was in space.

The tooth-billed pigeon, found on American Samoa, is the **OLDEST RELATIVE** of the extinct **DODO BIRD.**

DENIM

IS THE official fabric of California.

THERE IS A FLOATING POST OFFICE IN MICHIGAN.

A man in Florida drives a **cheeseburger-shaped** motorcycle.

A DJ in **New York City** helped create **hip-hop** music using a technique he called the **merry-go-round.**

INCLUDING ITS TERRITORIES, THE UNITED STATES SPANS

11 TIME ZONES.

50,000 YEARS AGO, A **METEORITE** THAT HIT WHAT IS NOW ARIZONA CAUSED AN EXPLOSION EQUAL TO **2.5 MEGATONS** (2,500 kilotons) OF **TNT.**

A **PAINTING** OF THE AMERICAN FLAG ONCE SOLD FOR $36 MILLION.

An American man who lived in a house **WITHOUT ELECTRICITY** until he was 14 created the first completely **ELECTRONIC TELEVISION SYSTEM.**

During the early Macy's Thanksgiving Day Parades, handlers let the balloons

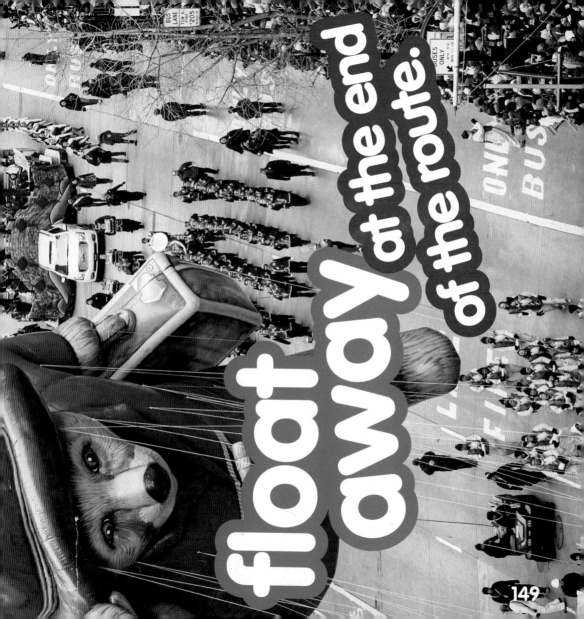

float away at the end of the route.

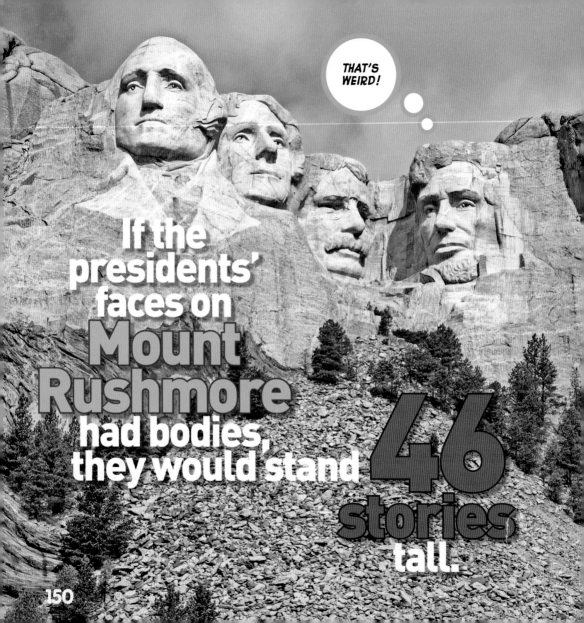

THE INFIELD OF THE INDIANAPOLIS MOTOR SPEEDWAY IN INDIANA COULD FIT 42 ROMAN COLOSSEUMS.

Every year, the **VALENTINE'S DAY "PHANTOM"** decorates businesses and homes in Montpelier, Vermont, with red **PAPER HEARTS.**

151

HAWAIIAN PIZZA WAS INVENTED BY A CANADIAN.

During World War II, performer Josephine Baker aided the Allies by writing messages in invisible ink on her sheet music.

Famous American cartoon character Scooby-Doo's full name is

Scoobert-Doo.

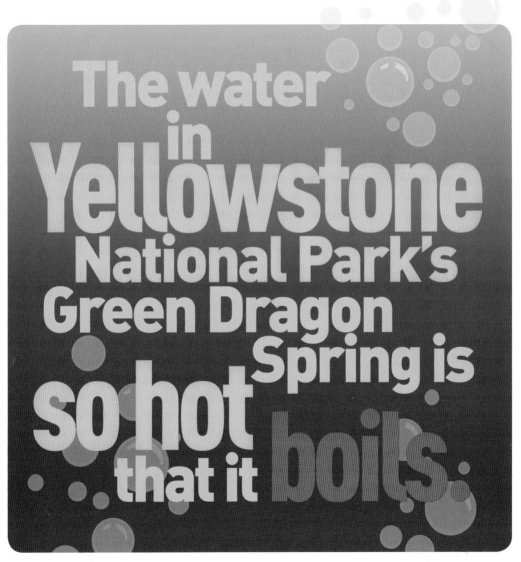

The water in Yellowstone National Park's Green Dragon Spring is so hot that it boils.

LINED UP END TO END, ALL THE ROADS IN THE UNITED STATES COULD CIRCLE EARTH 160 TIMES.

"Spambassadors" show visitors around a museum devoted to SPAM CHOPPED PORK AND HAM in Austin, Minnesota.

THREE BEARS BROKE INTO A COLORADO PIZZA SHOP AND WERE CAUGHT ON CAMERA EATING SALAMI AND DOUGH.

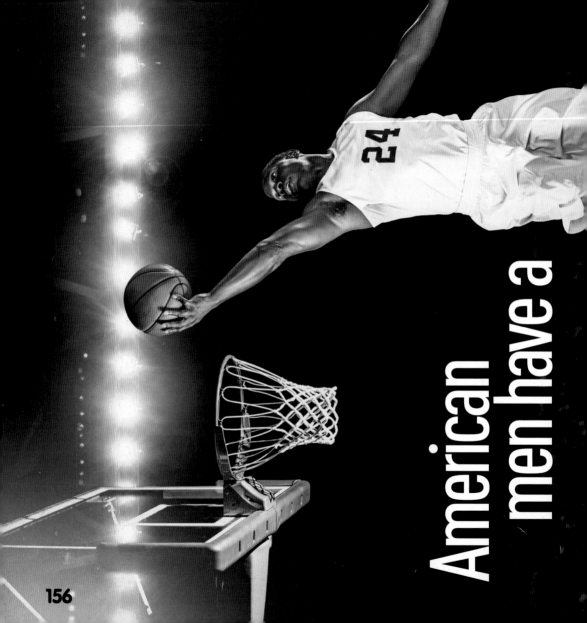

American
men have a

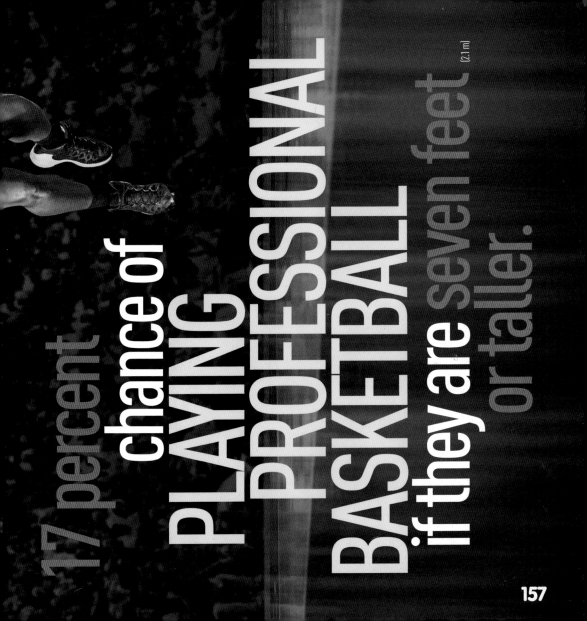

17 percent chance of **PLAYING PROFESSIONAL BASKETBALL** if they are seven feet [2.1 m] or taller.

157

An 11.5-foot-tall (3.5-m) **dinosaur** that roamed what is now North and South Dakota may have looked like a giant chicken.

Iowa is home to **Snake Alley**, **the most crooked street in the world.**

A **BISCUIT** IS THE **MASCOT** FOR A MINOR LEAGUE **BASEBALL TEAM** IN ALABAMA.

Minnesota was named the **happiest state** in the country.

159

According to New Jersey folklore, the **Jersey Devil** is a creature with the head of a goat, bat wings, and a forked tail.

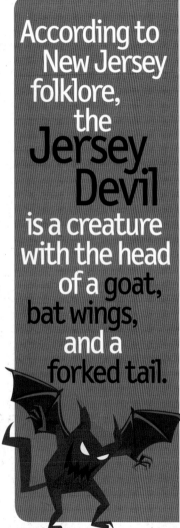

Thomas Edison invented a *sewing machine* powered by the human voice.

First Lady **MICHELLE OBAMA'S** Secret Service code name was **RENAISSANCE.**

THE **first shot** AMERICANS FIRED IN **WORLD WAR I** WAS IN **Guam**, A U.S. TERRITORY.

Sunken battleships FROM WORLD WAR I AND WORLD WAR II LIE **SIDE BY SIDE** IN **GUAM'S** HARBOR.

A CITY PARK IN PORTLAND, OREGON, IS LOCATED ON TOP OF A DORMANT VOLCANO.

Before they take office, POLITICIANS IN KENTUCKY must pledge that they have NEVER FOUGHT IN A DUEL.

First Lady **Eleanor Roosevelt** left a 1933 White House party to ride in a plane with **Amelia Earhart.**

A **restaurant** in Connecticut **gives away** three **FREE BOOKS** to **every customer.**

163

The North American short-tailed shrew paralyzes its prey with **venomous saliva.**

The streetlights on Hershey, Pennsylvania's Chocolate Avenue are shaped like Hershey Kisses.

Modern fortune cookies were first served in San Francisco by a Japanese-American chef.

U.S. astronauts' helmets have a piece of Velcro inside for scratching itches.

CALIFORNIA SEA OTTERS

have pouches under their arms for storing rocks, which they use TO OPEN CLAMS.

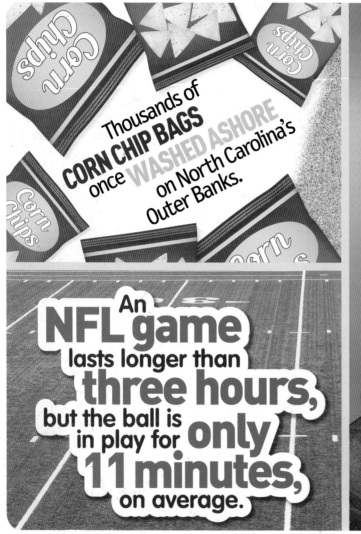

Thousands of **CORN CHIP BAGS** once WASHED ASHORE on North Carolina's Outer Banks.

An NFL game lasts longer than **three hours,** but the ball is in play for **only 11 minutes,** on average.

BENJAMIN FRANKLIN went door-to-door in Philadelphia to raise money for **STREET CLEANING.**

There was a
STAR WARS—
themed food truck
called the
GRILLENIUM
FALCON
in Fayetteville, Arkansas.

The **HOLLYWOOD** sign is as long as **FIVE BLUE WHALES.**

On his midnight ride, **PAUL REVERE** didn't shout "The British are coming"—he shouted **"THE REGULARS ARE COMING OUT."**

THE MERIWETHER LEWIS AND WILLIAM CLARK

EXPEDITION TO MAP THE AMERICAN WEST

COST 15 TIMES MORE THAN WHAT CONGRESS BUDGETED.

Utah's Rainbow Bridge, the world's longest natural bridge, is almost as long as a football field.

MAINE PRODUCES 90 PERCENT OF THE COUNTRY'S SUPPLY OF TOOTHPICKS.

AT A **skeleton museum** IN OKLAHOMA CITY, FLESH-EATING BEETLES ARE USED TO **clean** THE **bones.**

So many **butterflies** once migrated through Colorado that they showed up on a **weather radar map.**

When **Thomas Edison** needed a wheelchair, his best friend **Henry Ford** also got one so the two could *race.*

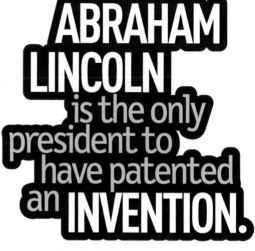

ABRAHAM LINCOLN is the only president to have patented an **INVENTION.**

In some 17th-century American colonies, it was **illegal to wear short sleeves.**

Montana's **Glacier National Park** has a canine **"bark ranger"** who helps keep wildlife away from visitors.

If you were to line up **all of Idaho's rivers** end to end, they would stretch longer than the width of the **United States.**

In about **15 million years,** some experts say, earthquakes will move **SAN FRANCISCO** and **LOS ANGELES,** California, **next to each other.**

A 58-foot (17.7-m) **STATUE OF A TERMITE** in Rhode Island is **928 TIMES LARGER** than the real insect.

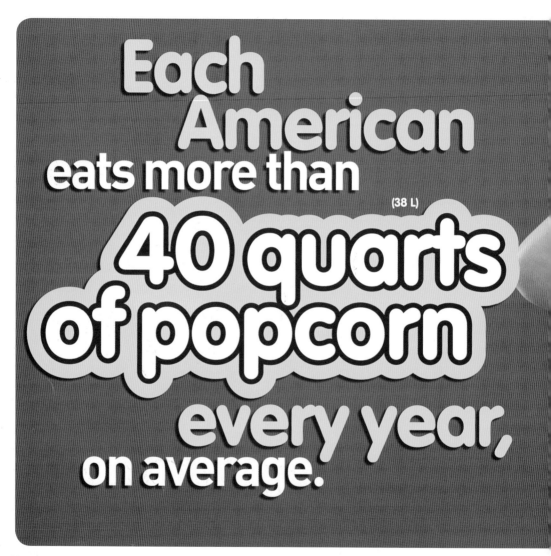

Each American eats more than (38 L) **40 quarts of popcorn** every year, on average.

The first American woman to **FLY A PLANE SOLO** never had a **FLYING LESSON.**

There are **more dogs than kids** living in Seattle, Washington.

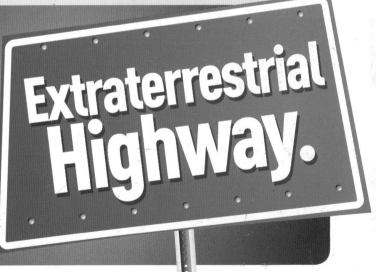

After many reports of alien sightings along a highway in Nevada, the state renamed it **Extraterrestrial Highway.**

THE U.S. POPULATION **INCREASES BY ONE PERSON** ABOUT EVERY **14** SECONDS.

A **GEYSER** in Yellowstone National Park is named **PUFF 'N STUFF.**

THE OFFICIAL CAR
OF THE U.S. PRESIDENT
IS NICKNAMED
THE BEAST.

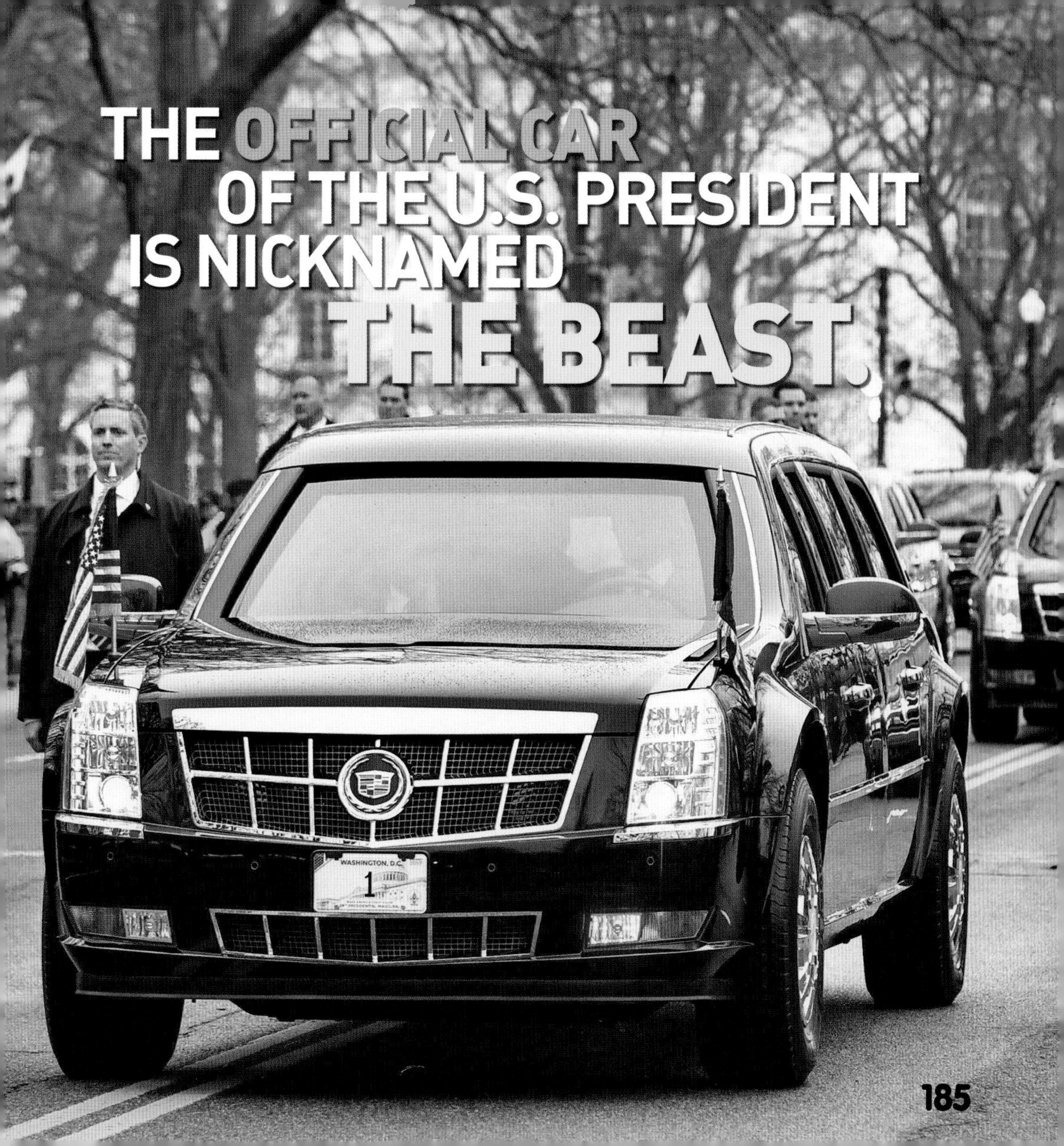

There's an
EIGHT-
HOLE
PUTTING
GREEN
at an airport in
Palm Beach,
Florida.

Massachusetts researchers created pasta that transforms into **3-D shapes** when dunked in water.

Some people in Portland, Oregon, tie **toy horses** to metal rings on curbs that were once used to secure **real horses and carriages.**

At New York City's **SEAGLASS CAROUSEL**, housed inside a glass-paneled shell, you can **RIDE ON A FIBERGLASS FISH.**

The United States **purchased Alaska** from Russia for $7.2 million— about **two cents** (0.4 ha) per square acre.

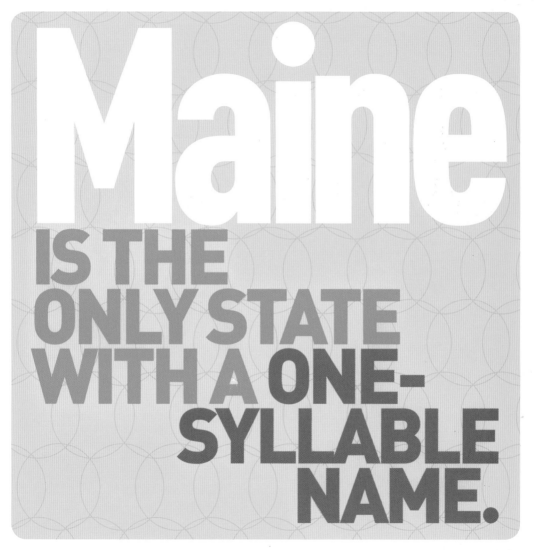

Maine
IS THE ONLY STATE WITH A ONE-SYLLABLE NAME.

All the bookshelves in the LIBRARY OF CONGRESS would stretch from DENVER, Colorado, to LOS ANGELES, California.

AMERICANS consume enough **peanut butter** every year to coat the floor of the **GRAND CANYON.**

A 1989 U.S. **SPACE SHUTTLE** MISSION ALMOST RETURNED TO EARTH BECAUSE

OUT OF ORDER

THE TOILET BROKE.

GOOGLE employees in Chicago, Illinois, can **PLAY VIDEO GAMES** at work.

Over the past 100 years,

HELLO, MY NAME IS

James

HELLO, MY NAME IS

and **Mary**

have been the **MOST POPULAR BABY NAMES** in the United States.

JOUSTING
is
Maryland's
official
STATE
SPORT.

THE "UNITED STATES OF EARTH." IN 1893, A CONGRESSMAN PROPOSED RENAMING THE U.S.A. THE

President **CALVIN COOLIDGE** sometimes **HID UNDER HIS DESK** to confuse his bodyguards.

A former NASA engineer built a **squirt gun** that can cut through a **watermelon.**

A pencil sharpener museum in Ohio has more than 3,400 sharpeners.

THERE ARE MORE MILES OF PAVED ROADS IN THE

Immigrants to **Ellis Island, New York,** were often **served ice cream** as part of their **first American meal.**

UNITED STATES THAN PEOPLE IN NEW MEXICO.

DURING **BRIDGE DAY** IN WEST VIRGINIA, **HUNDREDS OF PEOPLE** **PARACHUTE** FROM THE **875-FOOT-TALL** (267-m) NEW RIVER GORGE BRIDGE.

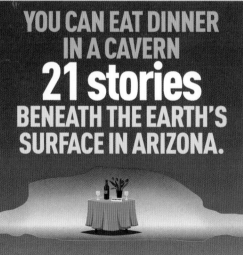

YOU CAN EAT DINNER IN A CAVERN **21 stories** BENEATH THE EARTH'S SURFACE IN ARIZONA.

A **house** in Rockport, Massachusetts, is **built** out of newspapers.

FACTFINDER

Boldface indicates illustrations.

A

Agriculture 55, **55**, 142, **142**
Airplanes 67, **67**, 182, **182**
Airports 23, **23**, 115, **115**, 186, **186**
Alabama 68, **68**, 159, **159**
Alaska
    diapers 91, **91**
    distance to Russia 7, **7**
    purchase price 188
    size 8, **8**
    transportation 132, **132**
    typing state name 114, **114**
Albany, New York 141
Aldrin, Buzz 104, **104**
Algonquian language 78
Alien sightings 37, 74–75, **74–75**, 183
Alligators **4**, 4–5, 30–31, **30–31**
"America the Beautiful" (song) 21
American bullfrogs 38, **38**
American flag 29, **29**, 147, **147**
American Revolutionary War 55, **55**, 132, **132**
American Samoa 60, 143, **143**
Apollo 10 lunar module 24, **24**
Arizona 41, 146, **146**, 199, **199**
Arkansas 60, **60**, 169
Arthur, Chester A. 53
Asheville, North Carolina 56–57, **56–57**
Astronauts 6, **6**, 104, **104**, 165, **165**
Atlanta, Georgia 23, **23**
Atoms 91, **91**
Aurora borealis 68, **68**
Austin, Minnesota 155

B

Baby names 192
Baker, Josephine 152
Bald eagles 3, **3**
Balloons 148–149, **148–149**
Baseball 121, 159, **159**
Basketball 41, **41**, 156–157, **156–157**
Batman 69, **69**
Bears 155, **155**
Beetles, flesh-eating 174, **174**
Berlin Wall 138, **138**
Bigfoot 112, **112**
Biking 132, **132**
Biltmore Estate, North Carolina 56–57, **56–57**
Biscuit, as mascot 159, **159**
Black cow (root beer float) 20, **20**
Blue crayons 136, **136**
Books 80, **80**, 126, **126**, 163, **163**, 190, **190**
Boston, Massachusetts 12, **12**, 51, **51**, 138
Bread 133, **133**
Breakfast 87, **87**
Bridge Day, West Virginia 199, **199**
Broccoli 67, **67**
Bullfrogs 38, **38**
Burgoo (stew) 138, **138**
Bush, George H. W. 67, 102, **102**
Butter 24, **24**
Butterflies 175, **175**

C

Calcium 65
California
    earthquakes 178
    fortune cookies 164, **164**
    Hollywood sign 170, **170**
    Los Angeles 21, **21**, 41, **41**, 58, **58**, 178
    Miss American Vampire 109
    Mono Lake 54, **54**
    official state dinosaur 119, **119**
    official state fabric 144, **144**
    rabbit playing basketball 41, **41**
    San Andreas Fault 39, **39**
    San Francisco 106–107, 107, 164, **164**, 178
    sea otters 166–167, **166–167**
    solar cells 83
    trees 42–43, **42–43**, 59, **59**
    UFO sightings 74, **74–75**
Camels 96, **96**
Candy **7**, 108, **108**
Captain EO (movie) 126
Cars 21, 109, **109**, 185, **185**
    see also Roads
Cartoons 152
Carver, George Washington 63, **63**
Casey, Illinois 34–35, **34–35**
Cats 9, **9**
Caves 52–53, **52–53**, 81, **81**, 199, **199**
Cheeseburger-shaped motorcycle 145, **145**
Chicago, Illinois 116–117, **116–117**, 134–135, **134–135**, 192
Chicken nuggets 113, **113**
Chickens 198, **198**
Chocolate factories 72, **72**
Christmas trees 98, **98**
Civil War, U.S. 125, **125**
Clark, William 171
Clinton, Bill 143
Coffee beans 55, **55**
Colonial America 7, **7**, 95, **95**, 176
Colorado
    butterflies 175, **175**
    cats 9, **9**
    dinosaurs 89, **89**
    State Fair 67, **67**
    UFO watchtower 37

201

Since 1888, the National Geographic Society has funded more than 12,000 research, exploration, and preservation projects around the world. The Society receives funds from National Geographic Partners, LLC, funded in part by your purchase. A portion of the proceeds from this book supports this vital work. To learn more, visit natgeo.com/info.

NATIONAL GEOGRAPHIC and Yellow Border Design are trademarks of the National Geographic Society, used under license.

For more information, visit nationalgeographic .com, call 1-800-647-5463, or write to the following address:

National Geographic Partners
1145 17th Street N.W.
Washington, D.C. 20036-4688 U.S.A.

Visit us online at nationalgeographic.com/books

For librarians and teachers: ngchildrensbooks.org

More for kids from National Geographic: natgeokids.com

For information about special discounts for bulk purchases, please contact National Geographic Books Special Sales: specialsales@natgeo.com

For rights or permissions inquiries, please contact National Geographic Books Subsidiary Rights: bookrights@natgeo.com

Designed by Chad Thomlinson

Library of Congress Cataloging-in-Publication Data

Names: National Geographic Kids (Firm), issuing body.
Title: USA/by National Geographic Kids.
Other titles: United States of America
Description: Washington, DC : National Geographic Kids, 2019. | Series: Weird but true | Includes index.
Identifiers: LCCN 2018031436| ISBN 9781426333712 (pbk.) | ISBN 9781426333729 (hardcover)
Subjects: LCSH: United States--Miscellanea--Juvenile literature.
Classification: LCC E180 .W45 2019 | DDC 973--dc23
LC record available at https://lccn.loc .gov/2018031436

The publisher would like to thank Julie Beer, researcher; Michelle Harris, researcher; Grace Smith, project manager; Paige Towler, project editor; Kathryn Robbins, art director; Hillary Leo, photo editor; Sarah J. Mock, senior photo editor; Alix Inchausti, production editor; and Anne LeongSon and Gus Tello, production assistants.

Printed in China
18/PPS/1

PHOTO CREDITS